What is... Sticky?

Heinemann

First published in Great Britain by Heinemann Library
an imprint of Heinemann Publishers (Oxford) Ltd
Halley Court, Jordan Hill, Oxford OX2 8EJ

MADRID ATHENS PARIS
FLORENCE PRAGUE WARSAW
PORTSMOUTH NH CHICAGO SAO PAULO
SINGAPORE TOKYO MELBOURNE AUCKLAND
IBADAN GABORONE JOHANNESBURG

© Heinemann Publishers (Oxford) Ltd

Designed by Heinemann Publishers (Oxford) Ltd
Printed in China

99 98 97 96 95
10 9 8 7 6 5 4 3 2 1

ISBN 0431 07976 5

British Library Cataloguing in Publication Data
Warbrick, Sarah
Sticky. - (What is...? Series)
I. Series
500

Acknowledgements
The Publishers would like to thank Toys Я Us Ltd,
the world's biggest toy megastore.,
for the kind loan of equipment and materials
used in this book.

Special thanks to Jodie, Katie, Michael, Nadia, Rose
and Winnie who appear in the photographs

Photographs: Bruce Coleman pp10, 11; NHPA pp8, 9;
other photographs by Trevor Clifford
Commissioned photography arranged by Hilary Fletcher
Cover Photography: Trevor Clifford

There are sticky things all around us.
Sticky things can be fun.
Sticky things can be useful.
Sticky things can also be messy!

This book shows you what is sticky.

These things look different.
What differences can you see?

In one way they are all the same.
They are all sticky.

Glue is very sticky.

Rose can stick things together with it.

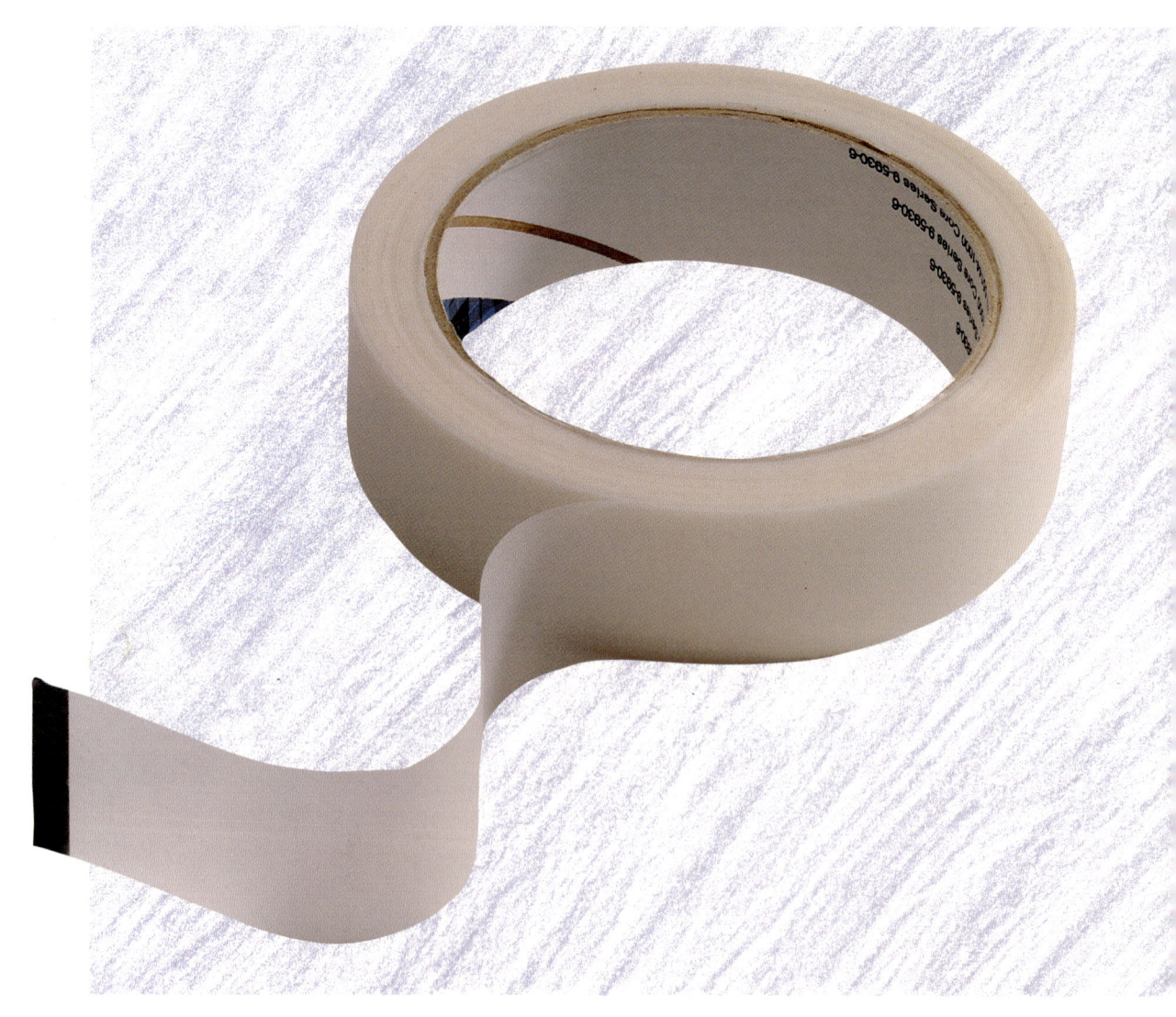

Sticky tape has glue on it.

What do you use it for?

Some seeds have tiny hooks on their surface.

They can stick to your clothes and to animals' fur.

The pollen from this flower sticks to the bee's legs.

The bee carries the pollen to another flower and it becomes unstuck.

These shoes have a special sticky fastener.

This makes them easy to put on and take off.

Mud can stick to your shoes.

But it can easily become unstuck on the carpet!

Pizza dough is sticky.

But look at it now it's cooked.

Sticky toffees can stick to your teeth.

Be careful!
Your teeth might come unstuck!

What is sticky here?

Index

bee 10, 11
glue 4, 5, 6
honey 2, 3
mud 14, 15
pizza 17
pizza dough 16, 17
pollen 10, 11
seed hooks 8, 9
'slime' 2, 3
sticky tape 6, 7
teeth 18, 19
toffees 18, 19